OUT
OF THE
PIT

OUT
OF THE
PIT

John W. Mount

ARPress
45 Dan Road Suite 5
Canton MA 02021

Hotline: 1(888) 821-0229
Fax: 1(508) 545-7580

Ordering Information:

Quantity sales. Special discounts are available on quantity purchases by corporations, associations, and others. For details, contact the publisher at the address above.

Printed in the United States of America.

ISBN-13:   Paperback   979-8-89356-013-8
              eBook   979-8-89356-014-5

Library of Congress Control Number: 2024902692

TABLE OF CONTENTS

DEDICATION

Dedicated to all the military veterans and others who suffer from the issues of depression, anxiety, and panic attacks.

"IN THE NAME OF JESUS CHRIST"

PROLOGUE

December 10th 1973. That was the day I surrendered my life to Jesus Christ. That made it possible for the Lord to show me whom I would marry, for man and wife are not to be unequally yoked. That's when one is saved by Christ and the other is not. This is a true story that began twenty nine years ago. Never would I have dreamed of such a "journey", because of my salvation. I must be clear before all, that I believe with all my heart and faith that everything written herein was necessary, for it was the means by which God chose to mold me into the Christian I am today-stronger, having a deeper faith; A faith that I apply to my life through the principles put forth in God's Word-the Holy Bible. *Romans 5:1-"Therefore being justified by faith, we have peace with God through our Lord Jesus Christ".* Truly I realize that God wanted me to become a man who can claim this verses as his own and live a truly committed life to Jesus Christ; It is a journey from darkness into light; A journey to a deeper, stronger, more committed faith; a faith that became completely dependent on God for even life itself.

AN ANXIOUS CALL

It all began with a phone call. 2 February 1991. The military operation Desert Storm was in full swing. I was the Administrative Sergeant doing normal daily duties at the Florida Army National Guard's 144th Transportation Company's unit's personnel office, which included answering the phone. The call came around 1030 hours (10:30 a.m.). "This is Sergeant Mount,

1SG Max L. Thomas

may I help you?" "This is Major X (I can't remember his name) from the 28th Transportation Battalion in Germany. Is your commander available? Hearing those words, I got a bad feeling in my stomach. "No sir Major, he's not available at this time". "Give him this message - I should have heard from him two weeks ago. As a matter of fact your unit should already be on the way here. Have him call me back". "Yes sir, as soon as possible sir". He gave me the overseas number for the return call. I felt a little worse. My fear had come true. Deployment during a wartime operation; separation from home, wife Linda & family with no guarantee of returning [alive]. To make matters worse, both of my sons were in the unit and would also be deployed. I got up with the First

Sergeant Thomas after he returned to the office and gave him the message. [First Sergeant Thomas (I called him Max when in an informal setting) was a former Marine Corps Drill Instructor at Paris Island. He loved life, his family, and always took care of his men, putting his needs last.] He then advised the commander Captain Lonnie Bradley.

This meant (1) official orders would soon be received from Army Command to deploy the unit overseas to a specific location, date of deployment, length of deployment, use of personal weapons, etc. and (2) I would have to make an administrative unit order to be signed by Captain Bradley and issued to each of the 185 unit personnel, including name, rank, and service number. These would be used along with individual military identification card (I.D. card) as needed by unit members while overseas. The ID card acts as passport for military members, and (3) the process of deployment of the unit would begin. That meant [I can't list them all] notification of all unit members, determining which, if any, members were not eligible for deployment, review and completion of deployment paperwork (such as DD Form 93-next of kin information, reviewing and updating any direct deposit forms for finances if needed, reviewing and updating legal documents such as wills, power of attorneys, guardianship for children, updating dental x-rays (for identification purposes if needed), dental exams performed and other administrative things.

The unit's equipment would be moved to a port to be shipped overseas prior to departure of the unit main body. Sergeant First Class Lewis, unit Supply Sergeant along with other chosen logistical personnel would depart early to arrange living quarters, arrival of equipment and move to the operations area, etc.

The unit was assembled and given briefings on the deployment and operation as information became available. Each person was given a diagram on exactly how to "pack" clothing and equipment for the flight overseas. Each backpack had to fit within "x" number of inches length and width and must fit inside a matching box. We had 72 hours to complete all necessary preparations, period. No one was allowed to leave the company area during this time until the evening of the day before separation.

The day before, my wife and I went to one of several church dinners and fellowships. Normally this was a happy time but for us it was very depressing. The church knew of my deployment tomorrow. After the meal the pastor and deacons took me to a quiet room where I knelt and received a "laying on of hands" while prayers were said over me for my well-being and for my wife. The annual festivities continued, then came to an end and we went home for one last night together. The date was 14 February 1991, Valentine's Day. We were to be gone for a year minimum.

The two of us at the Valentine's Day Dinner at the church the night before

On the third day, departure day, family members came to the unit for the deployment ceremony. Members met with family, husbands and wives renewed marriage vows, [I and my wife did this], speeches were made and long kisses. This was a somber time. All through this I was anxious, fearful and depressed. I did my best to hide these feelings.

Around mid-afternoon busses arrived to move the unit main body to a specified military deployment site. Even I, who am generally informed, because of my close work with the First Sergeant and Commander, was not aware of our destination which is rare. I guess most all members kissed family goodbye. As other members moved to the bus previously assigned to him or her [a point of clarification: actually two unit orders were made or "cut" by me. Each order had specific members on it. The reason is all command personnel cannot travel together in case of accident or occurrence. The commander on one bus and the First Sergeant on the other. Each order designated what bus/what plane specific members would ride on for safety reasons and coherence of unit leadership in case of accident.] I gave Linda the most heart-felt hug and kiss I had ever given. She and I walked to the bus together where I kissed her again. I wondered if I would ever see her again and was on the verge of tears. I could tell she was too. After the busses left my eyes were wet and I had a very difficult time staying my emotions but I did. Felt like the separation itself would kill me.

NEEDFUL PREPARATION

As we traveled we first stopped at a familiar place to rest/sleep and eat (called a RON-remain overnight). Camp Blanding Florida, a military training camp for most all military personnel (active duty, reserve, and national guard) in north east Florida. My unit had trained there many times, as well as army, navy, and marines. I don't think air force has trained there but they could have.

The next morning we loaded up and headed east to the Florida coast then north. Destination: Fort Stewart Georgia, a major mechanized infantry home (tanks) and a military deployment station. Hunter Airfield is located nearby where overseas flights depart from. Upon arrival at Stewart, we were taken to old World War II wooden open-bay barracks where we spent the next three weeks in "deployment readiness" activities. There were many other units there besides us. This "readiness" included refresher classes on nuclear, biological and chemical (referred to as NBC) actions (including going thru the dreaded "gas chamber" visit requiring exposure to CS gas), weapons qualifications, immunizations, dental checks, pre-deployment physicals, blood tests, eye exams, hearing exams. Also all the deployment paperwork on each member was checked again. Some of this was done in a gymnasium with different "stations" set up. Unit members went through in single file and stopped at each station (known as a "round robin) to be checked, poked, stuck with needles (immunized) [I was fortunate here, only had to have 8 shots, 4 in each arm-one after another], asked questions about insurance and finance etc. Anyway, after all said and done, I later found out due to proper prior planning, my unit completed all of its' "stations" faster than any other unit and set a base record for it. That made me very proud and pleased for the unit. As I said, we stayed there 3 weeks until we got the "green light" for overseas. During that time I found I was fighting depression and loneliness though I was not alone. I missed Linda terribly, but I did the old military thing: I sucked it up and drove on.

Waiting at Ft Stewart

As Administrative NCO I had to take care of any personnel issues that came up. A liaison non-com (NCO) was assigned to me to help me if needed. One of the unit members came and said his wife was sick and he needed a hardship discharge to be with her as a care giver. If this had happed during our initial 72 hours (as it should have been done) there would have been no problem. But, because it happened at Fort Stewart, this made my life much more difficult and stressful. It took me several days running around the base getting paperwork done to take care of this guy's problematic discharge and the liaison NCO who was supposed to help me did very little. Anxiety! Finally I got it done. End of that mountain climb.

In the last week at Stewart I was asked if I had the flight manifests for our personnel (one for each plane). All I had were the two unit orders I had cut. The liaison NCO said before we could board planes, we had to have a flight manifesto for each plane on a compact disc to be given to flight personnel. That meant I had to go to pre-flight area, use a small laptop and make each manifest with name, rank, and service number, again with zero..ZERO mistakes. Well, I was used to the zero mistakes thing, but I had little time to complete this as our flights were scheduled for the next morning. Pressure!!Anxiety! Using a laptop the keys of which my fingers would hardly fit. Stress! Okay. So I worked at it and got it done. End of the second mountain I had to climb at Fort Stewart.

CLOSE QUARTER FLIGHTS

The next day, we were herded onto the busses for a ride to Hunter Army Air Field where we loaded onto two Hercules C130 transport planes. These planes didn't have normal airline seats. They had aluminum tubing in 4 rows in the planes' cargo area. One row facing inward toward the center on the walls where the windows are and two rows down the center off the plane each row facing either outer row. I also seem to remember a few seats at the tail of the plane horizontally set, not many though. These seats were like sitting in a cramped armless nylon netting chair with about 18" width (or less). There was no support for the derriere, just a out space with nylon netting which was about 1" wide, red in color, all supported by 1 inch aluminum tubing. We loaded from the entrance door in single file moving to be back of the farthest row to the front, followed with each consecutive row until all four rows of seats were full. I was on the last row, outside wall where the plane door is, about 1/3rd of the way down from the door.

Now we weren't alone in those 18 inches. We all were wearing our web gear (fitted with canteen and gas mask) as well as our M16 rifle which had to be stowed behind us. Each person elbow to elbow, knee to knee. If people could be in a sardine can, this must be how it would be. The web seats could in no wise be called comfortable, in fact they were terrible. We were given meals during the flight with "exceptional" customer service which was don't-get-in-a-hurry-for-it. The flight crew started at the front of a row and handed individual meals out telling each row to "pass it down" to the last person in each row until everyone in the row had a meal. After eating, collection of meal containers was done the same way, only passing forward toward the front of the plane.

I didn't know this when it happened but after sometime in flight we had to land at Fort Dix, New Jersey. After disembarking, we had a time to relax, rest, eat a snack… whatever. Come to find out the first plane on which Captain Bradley was riding developed an engine problem and had to land either for repair or plane substitution; which one I never found out. I was able to call Linda; told her where I was and that I missed her and loved her. She said she was okay, but loved and missed me too. After a delay of about two hours, we were airborne again flying out over the Atlantic.

LANDING OVERSEAS

Rhine Mein Air Base, Germany. The total flight time was about fourteen hours. We disembarked and were told to get into company formation and drop our duffle bags and gear. Wait. While waiting I could see airport security with police dogs around other units. A lot of different things going on around me. The scene seemed strange-very different than what I was used to. I was very tired from the flight and know we all suffered from jet lag. All I could think about was getting some sleep but knew that wouldn't happen. Not yet. So here I was again in a situation and circumstance in which I had no control. [Note: I would later find out the issue of "no control" would play a more vitally important role in my life than it did at that time].

Now, onto the busses. The bus doors opened on the opposite side than those in the U.S. The bus driver was German and offered us soft drinks which was a pleasant surprise. The scenery was nice and the trip interesting enough. Certainly different from any scenery in the U.S. Sometime later, we went by a German prison which the driver remarked about. Not long after that we came to a fenced military compound with only one entrance through guard posts [This compound was not a military base].

This compound was Spinelli Barracks, the home of the 28th Transportation Battalion in Mannheim, Germany [also FRG, the Federal Republic of Germany]. Past the entrance gate and guard check point, there were buildings on the left and right, then a large courtyard like opening on the right with a large three story building centered on the courtyard. There were two other three-storied buildings set on each side of the courtyard perpendicular to the center building forming a sort of square horseshoe. The one on the left was a transportation company. The one on the right side past the gate was the post office and barber shop. In the same building after were company barracks and administrative offices, and again a mess hall for a different transportation company. If standing in front of the large centered building (which turned out to be the compound headquarters' building, there was a gymnasium across the entrance road from the gate. This road made a large u turn around what looked like storehouses or garages of some sort. After making the last left turn going back toward the entrance road, were a small café on the right, then another barracks building which became the new home of the 144th Transportation Company. There was another building in the far right top corner of the courtyard which was a snack bar. The compound itself was enclosed by a two mile perimeter of chain link security fencing set in the shape of a square. I knew this because the first time the unit did early morning PT (physical training) we had to run around the outside of it, beginning to the right outside the gate and ending with a right turn inside the gate. There was no other open entrance that I knew of. There were other areas such as a motor pool where the vehicles were kept, as well as driver training sections for refreshing driver abilities. I never saw these.

My new world was of the barracks, the office, and other buildings I frequented in the performance of my duties. The buildings were concrete. Smooth fascia, three stories, a partial basement [I say that because the only thing I ever saw on that level was the unit supply room area which was down steps to the left of the front doors], and attic. The attic had one or two rooms for sleeping Also a large section used as a rec room or conference room with a flag painted on the wall. To my knowledge nobody went up there. The first floor was the dining room on the right by the entrance doors, a short hallway and

In the admin office.

rooms for women' quarters. Stairs. Second and third floors were rooms for men's' quarters. The commander and staff were housed in a separate building from the company. The third floor had offices too, down the hallway on the right to room with several desks, filing cabinets, one television which got one channel (Armed Forces Network, Germany), a coffee pot that didn't work on a brown wooden table, and a smaller office on the left which was the unit commander's office. There were regular small brass mailboxes with combination dials for mail on the right of the door and a small open area behind them for sorting mail to individuals.

Most rooms had bunks for two to four people (could have been five but can't remember). The rooms locked from the inside but could only be opened by a key from the outside, the number of which depended on the number of people assigned to the room. Each bunk had its' own wall locker and storage space. My room was a two person room and was close to the office, as that would be my base of operations every day. Fortunately I had the room to myself which I was very thankful for. God always works things out.

Each room was heated by steam regulator but it put out little heat even in the wide open position. I normally slept in Army issued long underwear with a knit hat on because the rooms were never really comfortable to me. Two swing out windows above the radiator had a window ledge big enough to sit on. Also each room had a small refrigerator maybe 30" high, with two shelves and a very small freezer on top. One door.

Even though it's not spring yet, the night (after 10pm) wasn't dark. Seems enough light remained to see by. I found this strange.

A few words on why we were at Spinelli. A trucking company had been deployed from Spinelli to Qatar or somewhere in the Middle East. Our unit was to replace that unit to continue its' work while they were gone. That meant transporting food and equipment, ammunition or wheat ever was needed at other locations within the country. As a note (which I didn't find out for several months) we were on schedule to rotate to the Middle East to swap assignments with the company we replaced, thus giving them a return to Spinelli.

Everything got unloaded, the office set up, and I and my very capable assistant Sergeant Brenda Richert settled in along with the First Sergeant. There was one large double window in the center of the outside wall from which we could see the snow- capped mountains. One of the first things she and I did after settling in was to attempt to fix the coffee pot. Several attempts were made but to no avail, so after a few days

13

we pooled some money and bought a new one. That coffee pot was a real friend to us during our stay there. The only problem for me was there was no creamer or sugar at first and that meant black coffee. Thankfully that issue was also resolved.

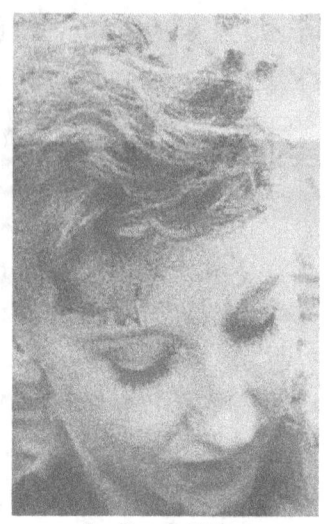

Sgt Brenda Richert

I and Sergeant Richert had multiple duties within the office area. She handled distribution of the mail every day. I did personnel reports to the battalion every day which consisted of how many people were present, who was sick or those with health issues; who was not able to do their duties because of doctor appointments (sick call) or other things. These reports were done with an army system called SIDPERS. It was not an issue for me to do it, but I was the only person in the company who had training on it and knew how to do it. I and Sergeant Riker handled daily correspondence, manning the telephones, taking and giving messages, filing. Whatever needed doing. Mostly each day was going through the motions and passing time.

In the evenings (8:00pm) I would venture to a single pay phone by the post office where I would call Linda. It was always really good to talk with her as I thought of her during each day multiple times…staying at home by herself, no one to help her, out in the country, taking care of our dogs; Is she well, is the car ok, is she safe?? I worried about her but could do nothing. On the calls I did my best to be positive and lift her up just as she did me, and we said we missed and loved each other, but in reality there could be no change in the separation from her without God's help. No change unless he intervened and caused a change. Prayers for her and about the separation were very frequent. Each of us could only trust in the Lord and wait with patience for his deliverance from our being apart.

We had been married seventeen years and our anniversary occurred apart. It was the hardest anniversary we ever had. But a good thing happened for it. Fortunately each weekend office personnel had the two days off. I and many other unit members learned of the excellent rail system available to travel the miles into Mannheim proper.

The city was set up like a chessboard in blocks. Once we figured that out we could navigate around the town pretty well. From the train station I would travel "north" [may not have been but that's the way I laid out the city grid squares in my head] – walking of course. There was a large open "square" with a recognizable architecture, and in the middle a very beautiful ornate water works

Linda and the Spanish Black Lamb coat.

fountain. Brick streets with trolley car tracks going down the middle of streets - All kinds of shops on each side with many prohibiting vehicles. One great thing about these were the bread shops. Large round loaves with very crispy outside and soft inside. Delicious! Leaving the "fountain" square walking north again I came to an "open" market. A market with canvas/material covering each sellers' wares which were greatly varied - food, coffee, vegetables, lots of stuff. One day I went to the north of the market and looked to the right down the street. Many German shops display merchandise outside, and I saw a shop with coats hanging out front. Walked to it and looked at them —furs, and all on sale! I couldn't speak German and the elderly shopkeeper didn't speak English but we managed to make a deal. I bought a waist length black Spanish lamb coat for Linda and was excited about mailing it to her for our anniversary. I called her and told her to expect a package. About two weeks later I got a letter from her with a picture of her and the coat. She loved it but wished I could have been there to see her open it. It was one of the few bright times of this deployment.

For the most part each day was going through the motions, doing what needed to be done. I did enjoy going into Mannheim on weekends but didn't go on any touring jaunts to other towns or cities to visit castles and historical sites. Sometimes I stayed in quarters and read.

One morning an odd thing happened. I woke up normally and sat up. Immediately the room was spinning very fast in a counter clockwise motion. I tried standing up but couldn't without holding onto something. I was suddenly very nauseous and had to get to the latrine (bathroom) located on the left at the end of the hall. I leaned against the concrete wall and every door on my way there where I got sick. The problem was this didn't go away. I managed to get to the office and after a few minutes wait had a driver and a vehicle to take me to Ben Franklin Village, the much larger military complex with most everything regular U.S. bases had. The drive over was horrendous with me very dizzy and the truck moving. Got to the infirmary, the driver helped me walk in and I was seen by a doctor. After his check- up, the diagnosis was extreme vertigo due to something called Meniere's disease. I was given antibiotics and an anti-dizziness script called Meclizine. He said mine was the worst case of vertigo he had ever seen. Back at the barracks I stayed in bed getting up only if necessary for two weeks. When I got to the point I could get up and walk without help I went back to duty but carefully. I began to learn about head and eye movements that aggravated the condition. Going down the stairs was a challenge. The dizziness gradually subsided to a somewhat tolerable level but even with that I was nauseous most of the time. Limiting my movements whenever possible became a necessity.

Everything pretty much stayed status quo. Several of us had started a bible study group which helped us spiritually. I continued to pray for deliverance from this situation every day. Finally in mid-May we got news that we were scheduled to rotate to the Middle East the first week in June and the original company there would return to Spinelli. This had not been released to the company but Captain Bradley, First Sergeant Thomas and I were aware of it, along with Sergeat Richert. However, I can happily say that God answered my prayer. The situation in the Mideast has changed drastically and within another week we officially received orders we would be returning stateside within one week. Praise the Lord! Necessary logistics were accomplished, the barracks cleaned, mattresses rolled and onto the busses for the airport. I was still having vertigo issues (from what I term as "residuals" from the onset of the disease) and was very anxious due to the vertigo about the flight home.

At the airport we went through military customs. The company was briefed on banned items that could not be taken onboard the plane. Each soldier went into a "disposal area", a curtained private area in which was one item: a garbage can. Anybody with a banned item had to put it in the can because after exit from the area, military police would randomly pick someone to inspect their baggage. A short distance from each disposal area stood the MP at a "check out" counter. If chosen you were ordered to dump (empty) duffle bags on the counter for inspection as well as (in my case) brief cases or hand-carried bags. I had no banned item and proceeded to be checked out. I got picked. I had my duffle bags and administrative briefcase. These were heavy enough but each of us were also wearing web gear, gas mask and M16. With the residual vertigo all this made a difficult go for me [I weighed an in-shape 135 pounds and was walking with at least 100 pounds or more). I got picked. I set the briefcase and duffle bags down. Upon unlocking my clothing bag the first thing the MP saw were the feet of a foot high blue and white stuffed bunny which Linda has sent me. It was the last thing and the top thing in the duffle bag. I don't know to this day why except it must have been the Lord looking out for me, but after I took the bunny out the MP looked at it and said never mind. No need to dump it..Go ahead. God does help us even in very small ways. What a relief. I was sweating and walking a bit wobbly and got to go sit down for a while. Hooray!

The wait for the plane was a couple of hours. Finally we all boarded the plane, but this time to our surprise, we had airline seats. The long flight back to the states would be better.

RETURNING HOME

The flight went smoothly and my vertigo was manageable, eventually landing back at Hunter after a refueling stop then busses to Fort Stewart. There we underwent physicals for any health issues prior to release to return to home station. Several of our guys had hernias, a couple had some back/ spine issues from injuries and they had to stay for surgeries or treatment for another two or three weeks before being released. Seven I think opted to stay on and remain on active duty. Guess they liked it. Me, I wanted to get back home to Linda. Couldn't get there fast enough. We loaded on busses again and left Fort Stewart headed south. The date was May 22nd 1991 give or take a day. The busses arrived home two days later.

The arrival was a happy day. The city had organized for us to parade through town with people cheering and glad to have us home. We underwent some welcome home speeches. All the while I wanted this to end so I could go home. At one point wives go tired of waiting and moved into our formation to stand by husbands, Linda included. It was a happy, very thankful time for God had done what many said couldn't happen. One year at least. God had intervened and brought us home early! When released I and a few other active duty unit members had three weeks leave before returning to our normal duties. When I walked in house the feeling was strange, like seeing it for the first time, all new, neat and comfortable. After the leave time, I returned to duty and all went smoothly until August of 1992.

LEAVING AGAIN

August is in the middle of hurricane season in Florida. Walking in the door after church on Sunday 23 August 1992 a message was on the answering machine. It said, get your stuff and report for duty. This meant I had to leave-*again*. After the unit assembled, I kissed Linda goodbye and got on bus. The emotional pain I had felt from last year came back but not so hard. This time we were headed to Miami to give help to those devastated by category 5 Hurricane Andrew and not going overseas. We arrived Monday afternoon, after staying in Ocala overnight. The location was Tamiami Park off of Tamiami Trail. This was a park with a large multifaceted building. Each company had its' own section.

We got to work. The drivers went to a marshaling area and picked up the unit equipment. I and the First Sergeant set up the administrative area which was a folding table or two with folding chairs. I had my old dependable Remington manual typewriter. There was no electricity, no lights. The bathroom was a small commercial type bathroom that came with the added luxury of a few inches of water in the floor. Running water was available. Thankfully, my unit had a mess (food service) section which cooked our meals, one breakfast, one dinner. Lunch was individual MRE (Meal, Ready to Eat). Folding cots were obtained and a section of our area set up for sleeping by platoons. 1-Headquaanrters (administrative functions, communication) 2-Driver Platoon 3-Driver Platoon and 4-Maintenance (vehicle care, portable lighting, etc). We each had a sleeping bag to roll out on the cot. I had brought and eggshell foam pad which I used and was thankful for. I managed to obtain a few plastic milk cartons which I stacked at the head of my cot as storage shelving for books, personal items etc. The only "luxury" we got was a portable 13" television and VCR player with some movies which we made full use of after the power was restored. There were a couple of picnic benches we made use of for sitting around, eating on or watching a movie.

Each day work assignments were given and unit members went to it. They distributed bottled water, food, and other items needed by the public, cut up trees, removed storm debris; Anything that was needed as we were able to perform for the aid of people devastated by this massive storm. My duties were as when overseas: daily strength reports, mail, and this time payroll. I stayed at Tamiami while drivers and maintenance members ventured out to assist. One thing I will say, one thing the aftermath of the storm provided were great amount of large mosquitos and flying bugs. They were terrible. The heat was also bad. Rain too, as if we needed more.

As the days and weeks passed there were other units providing voluntary support of our unit mission. These guys were temporarily assigned to our unit. Unfortunately for me that meant I had to do payroll for my unit as well as for these temporary duty personnel which came from ten other units. Name, rank, service number, unit name individually typed in multiple copies, line by line, on a manual typewriter without mistakes. That was my most daunting tasks.

This mission continued, not for weeks, but months. In the first week of October some units were starting to be released by the Governor. It was a slow process as the need was so great. We were one of the last units to be released to return home which occurred in November. I also had to insure mail in voting ballots were completed and mailed for the general state election in early November for all unit members. Again I faced the separation in some depression but kept busy; always thinking of *Linda home alone, Again*. It was wonderful when I got back home but I'll admit I had some back pain for a while after sleeping or trying to sleep on those folding cots for three months.

INTO THE PIT

Christmas came and went, then New Year's 1993. I was 43 years old. Each New Year's day I do two things: 1) the first thing I say after midnight or when I wake up (if I don't stay up to see in the new year) is "Rabbit, Rabbit, Rabbit".

This both I and my sister Suzy have done for years and continue to do. Its' origin is from our grandfather C. D. Flynt who was one quarter part Cherokee Indian. Maybe it was like Roosevelt's "a chicken in every pot" thing, but we never really knew. Just something he did and it got passed on to us as a tradition and (2) I pray, give thanks to God for the New Year and ask His blessings on our home and family. He has always provided our needs (especially life needs as food, bills paid, transportation, and roof over our heads). *"For my God shall supply all your needs according to his riches in glory by Christ Jesus"*(Phillipians 4:19).

At this point I will break from 1993 to return 44 years into the past. Enter the verses Isaiah 55:8-9. *"For my thoughts are not your thoughts, neither are your ways my ways, saith the Lord. For as the heavens are higher than the earth, so are my ways higher than your ways and my thoughts higher than your thoughts"*. This is an unusual verse to use at this time but it is a profound statement about how God works in the lives of individuals for what is to follow so keep it in mind. Our family didn't understand it, and had to live out its' effects from then own.

Living in Florida we loved to swim. In the summer of 1957 I was 6 years old, my sister Suzy was 8 and my brother Jimmy was 11. Some people said he could swim like a fish and could hold his breath underwater a long time. The three of us were at the city swimming pool. We would spend the entire day at the pool when we went there. [We did swim in the local lake a lot because our grandfather had built a home on it which was, to my knowledge the first one-completed in 1952.] Near closing time everyone was ordered out of the pool so the pool could be drained (and cleaned?). One of Jimmy's friends (his age) had a silver dollar. For some reason he threw it in the pool (the depth was 10 feet) and dared Jimmy to dive in and get it. He could keep it if he did. Well, Jimmy took the dare. Unfortunately the pool drain had already been opened and he was sucked into the drain opening. The life guard took action and emergency personnel were called. The suction was too great. It took about two hours for divers to free his body. I remember being there but mostly I have suppressed the details of the memory. I know my father became an alcoholic after Jimmy's death and remained so for many years. He regained sobriety in the early 1980s but it made for a difficult life at times. He was, however, no matter how drunk, always loving and never got mad or abusive of any of us.

As days passed I knew Jimmy was dead. His best friend, a boy his age named Jerome Taylor came to see if I would like to spend the night at his house. He would take me to the movie theater to watch whatever was playing while he worked part time as an usher. It became a regular thing, and very good for me at the time. We walked to the Ritz Theater about a mile from his house and walked in. No payment needed. I watched every western, action, mystery, science fiction and horror movie shown, but I had to sit in the very back row and not walk around. In the 1950s movies were black and white. I grew to love them, especially science fiction, and horror: giant spiders, monsters, outer space creatures, invaders to earth. Boris Karloff, Christopher Lee, Vincent Price, Peter Cushing all became my favorites. Lee & Cushing came in the late 50s-in color. I still watch and enjoy those old classic movies today.

At the time I never thought about *"why"* I grew to love them but now some 60 years later I came to know why and how they impacted my character as an adult. The reason? I wanted to see the good guys win, the bandit caught, the monster destroyed, the invader defeated, even evil itself vanquished by the power of good. And now, especially the demons of the subconscious that caused the depression and anxieties I was now battling.

Back to the New Year1993. My father had retired from business management and was doing taxes for local businesses and individuals to keep busy. My grandmother (Mimi) lived alone as her husband (Pawpaw) had died in November 1974. In the spring of that year she had a stroke and needed help in the home. Daddy went to her house during the day and worked from there. One day she fell and Daddy had a time getting her up and into bed. For several weeks after that he used Bengay on his back as he believed he had strained muscles picking her up. Mimi had to go into a nursing home very soon after that. Daddy didn't go to the doctor unless he was really sick. Well, finally he was taken to be examined by his doctor and the doctor immediately ordered him in hospital for treatment of lung cancer. This was June 24. [He had been a smoker many years and had successfully quit in 1981 or 82]. This cancer came as a great shock to all of us. The family was very worried and depressed. We visited him in a stepdown room when he asked us "who was that man in the white coat?" No one was in the room but us. *God had started showing him things.* Afterwards he was moved to a private room. We each took turns staying with him around the clock. One day Linda was with him. She was reading but noticed he was awake and looked as if he was seeing something in the distance. He told Linda "read your book" but also said "don't worry, John will find a good job in Marianna", which was strange as I had an excellent job in the Guard with a long future. He died 13 days after admission, one week before his 78th birthday. Daddy was the smartest man I ever knew, a mental mathematical wizard, and the very best father any son could have in spite of the alcoholism. He was my only hero when he died. Separation anxiety and depression again. I also learned that periods of stress and anxiety triggered my vertigo.

Now here's the strange thing about what he said. The following October my active duty position came under scrutiny (as did all other such positions in Florida) and was to be eliminated in a military Reduction in Force economic action by the state. I resigned effective 15 January 1994 and used my separation leave for three months. My discharge came effective 24 March 1994 after nearly 22 years of military service. *This is what God had shown Daddy in the hospital just before his death.* This resulted in a period of non-employment of about eighteen months. Devastatingly long for a man who believed in providing for family, taking care of wife, hearth and home. This upholds a man's self- esteem and feeling of worth. I had none at this point and was very depressed. I spent a lot of time in prayer begging God to help. A lot of time searching for meaningful work. I wanted something in an administrative area as I had in the military, but God closed every door. One day I cried unto the Lord "be merciful Father, give me a job, any job-something". Not long after I got a part time job doing invoicing for a local dry cleaner. My first paycheck was about $35. I kept praying and looking for better opportunities.

After this I worked full time as a service writer in a local car dealership. This taught me customer skills. Some mechanics there said I should be the next Service Manager. But again, God works in mysterious ways. I worked in that position for five months when an irate customer complained and I would be let go in two weeks, allowing me a short time to find something else. It was October 12th 1995. Fear/Anxiety/Depression attacked again. But this time, something else – *God's intervention in my personal life.*

My wife did opening remarks for Sunday school and said something has helped me more than once: "FEAR knocked [on your door], FAITH answered [the door]. NO ONE there [when the door was opened].

After being told I was to be let go I heard from someone at the dealership that an old friend of my father's and myself [known as "Buddy Rooks" needed help at another dealership. Buddy was a well- known and respected Christian man who worked in auto mechanics in the neighborhood of 45 years. He was the Service Manager.

FAITH was with me this time. I drove over, talked with him and he hired me on that day. I went back to the other dealer and told the owner I wouldn't be needing his two weeks. Again *"But my God shall supply all your needs according to His riches in glory by Jesus Christ"* (Phillipians 4:19).

GOD PROVIDES THE JOB

"Assistant Service Manager" was the official title of the position. For the first six months to a year I disliked the job. There were people who complained a lot and there were people who were very nice. It's difficult to like someone who always looks at the negative. I learned why good customer relations skill is important; why being friendly, courteous, and compassionate for customers problems can bring reward. I took a look at attitude and this came to mind: *"And the Lord said, I am Jesus whom thou persecutes: it is hard for thee to kick against the pricks"* (Acts 9:5). I realized I had been fighting the job, kicking against the bad of it, which was a poor attitude for the position God had given me. I prayed "Father, forgive me for my attitude. I surrender this job and myself unto Thee, ask that You help me, guide me, and make of this what your will is". Immediately after praying that I had peace about the job, the work to do in it, and the results of it. The complaining customers mostly disappeared, though there were some difficult ones I always seemed to be assigned to take care of. But that didn't bother me either. I learned to live this verse: **Luke 6:31** *"And as ye would that men should do to you, do ye also to them likewise"*. These words became my guide and I applied them every day. That's why those difficult customers weren't so difficult for me. One day into the next into the next. I prayed with customers, I prayed for their cars. Every day the same and every day different. As time went by more customers were writing letters – good letters- to the owner about the service department and me. Many customers thought I was the service manager but never was and didn't seek the position. I was satisfied where I was and got satisfaction from helping people – doing whatever I could to solve their car issues.

MORE ATTACKS AND DEPRESSION

During this period (can't recall the year), maybe 2005, I got a call from Linda while I was working saying she had fallen and gotten hurt. I drove home and found her in a lot of pain. She'd fallen off a step ladder. Strangely enough it was because one foot of the ladder was on top of an underground burrow made by a rabbit or armadillo, and as she started to climb down, the foot sank in toppling the ladder. It went one way and she went the other. She told me as she was falling everything went dark-her eyes were open-and she heard a voice tell her *"Linda, you're falling. Cross your arms over your chest"* which she did. She said it was a long time before she hit the ground as if time had stopped. We found out she had broken her back in two places. She had to stay reclining either on the couch or bed for four to six months. She healed slowly but eventually was able to get up, walk, and even drive though she had and still has trouble looking behind her when reversing. Because of her inactivity for such a time she put on some weight and developed type 2 diabetes. All through this my old fear, anxiety and depression paid me a visit. Linda was pretty depressed too and in a lot of pain. She had always been very active and enjoyed her gardening and flowers, shopping etc. She now couldn't do all that so she too was depressed. Even now she fights depression and pain from her fall. We don't know why she had to fall but feel it was God's will that it happen.

As for me, I started going to the Veterans Administration for my healthcare as I hadn't had any health insurance since March of 1991. I developed some health issues and needed help. I got up early (4:30) each day for work so I went to bed early (9:00). Started waking up feeling tired. Didn't have much energy. Also noticed (as time passed) that anytime Linda said "I hate to tell you this but…" my arms started to burn. Once a neighbor came to install an ice maker line to the fridge and at first it leaked a little at a connection. I was watching. Immediately I felt a wave of heat flow through my body from my head down. My arms felt as if they were on fire, my breathing got faster, and I felt bad fatigue and nausea as well as shaking-had to go lie down. I talked with the doctor about the burning and he gave me a script for nerve pain. I took that for a three year period during which I developed severe fatigue. I diagnosed it as chronic fatigue syndrome, but my doctor never told me he had diagnosed it as that.

The fatigue worsened. Each day I got up just as tired as I was when I went to sleep. My sleep was not good. Went to sleep fine but woke up every 1.5 to 2 hours. Sometimes it was difficult to get back to sleep. Nightmares of a military nature had started; Mostly I was overseas and couldn't get back home. Most were not violent but many times they would wake me up scared, not sure of where I was for a second. Then I would think or whisper "you're ok John, you're home in bed, you're home". I would pray and ask God to stop the bad dreams-give me good enjoyable dreams. I got to the point where I told the doctor that at bed time I thought "just scrape me off the floor with a shovel and carry me to the bed" because I was that fatigued. When I got up I had to mentally make myself get up and go to work because I had no energy. I wanted to do something in the yard but couldn't so I hired a friend who was out of work to do the job. This was something I had never done.

I kept having the burning in my arms, the nausea and the weakness if I even thought something was going bad; Thought I had developed fibromyalgia and saw a neurologist. His report was negative. I had a painful nerve induction test and a bone marrow biopsy. Tests inconclusive. My doctor recommended me to see the VA psychiatrist but I declined this at first. When my symptoms didn't get better, I told the doctor and he gave me some more scripts after bloodwork. Eventually the fatigue issue started improving but the burning, weakness and nausea issues did not. Again, they got worse. The depression was really kicking in. As it grew worse I tried to hide it.

I went day to day trying to fight it off but my mental state got lower and lower until I got where I was in a deep, dark pit. I mentally looked up and could see no light. The walls were smooth. There was no way out.

This depression was absolutely crushing. It effected my work – customers knew something was wrong. It effected my relationship with Linda. I started treating her mean, pulling away, making choices like refusing to do dishes anymore or helping out at home. This was the hardest time on me and on Linda as well. I distanced myself from her and turned into myself, not wanting to go to church, to socialize, or see other people. It was absolutely horrible. I didn't know what to do. I had no peace. I was at war within my body and within my mind.

I had been doing the only thing I knew how to do-pray. I "prayed without ceasing" as Paul wrote and continually asked God to help me. No answers. No guidance. Absolutely no hope. Just deeper and deeper.

Eventually I had to accept reality. *I concluded my subconscious mind was over-reacting to situations and circumstances that caused fear within me.* My body's reaction to bad news, to the perception of something going wrong - anything - was so bad I was like an alcoholic or drug addict being controlled by it not the other way around, the normal way. I told doc I was tired of being controlled by whatever was causing these issues and I wanted to get help. I accepted the referral and I went to my first appointment with the psychiatrist. After I answered some questions on Post Traumatic Stress, depression, and anxiety she looked over the answers. We talked. *The diagnosis was Generalized Anxiety Disorder with Acute Panic Attacks and Depression.* I did learn that clinical depression can exist without a person feeling depressed. Some symptoms are fatigue, lack of motivation, poor sleep or insomnia. The cause? *Separation Anxiety.* Finally a diagnosis. **She told me "The Enemy Is Fear".** She started me on some anti-anxiety/depressants and I took them for several years; different ones at different times finding which suited me best.

I remembered what Linda said in the Sunday school opening about fear knocking, faith answering, and no one was there.

Years earlier when my brother died. I think that started it all. At the age of 6 my mind suppressed what happened but *my subconscious interpreted the incident – and this is key – as one in which I had no control over my circumstances.* After a lifetime of attacks I felt hope.

HOPE AND CLIMBING OUT

One Friday in August I got a phone call from a customer I had seen perhaps two times. Didn't really know him and certainly didn't recognize him. He needed an oil change on his truck and wanted to come in Monday to get it done. The next part of the conversation completely floored me. He said *"God has put you hard on my mind for the last two weeks. I know something is wrong and I want a private talk with you so I will know how to pray for you"*.

No one I knew had spoken to him. I certainly didn't tell him. I have trouble trusting people and I would never reveal my personal issues with someone I don't trust. I keep my thoughts and feelings to myself. This provides me with a barrier of safety from people. I pondered that phone call all weekend and was ready to meet him on Monday. His name is Major. When he arrived I did my thing to get his truck into service and we had our conversation. After I explained what I was going through he said *"You may not believe this but I am going through the same thing – now.* While the truck is being serviced I'm going to walk around the parking lot praying for you – asking God for an answer or guidance". The temperature outside was above 95 degrees. He walked and prayed and talked with God. When he was done, he came in sweaty but in good spirits. He said "don't worry. God will answer your prayers and bring you out". We both knew God had sent this good Christian man to help me through by God's counsel. [Since then we have become good friends, brothers in Christ who fought the same battles. We call each other to check on each other and pray for any needs].

When I heard him say that I felt a great surge of hope, power, goodness come over me. I had finally received the rope dropped into the pit with which I could begin the journey to climb out. And it was a journey. I continued reading my bible (1611 King James Version) and came across Psalm 37. Reading it hit me like a hammer. **Psalm 37:3-7 (3) *"Trust in the Lord and do good; so thou shalt dwell in the land, and verily thou shalt be fed. (4) Delight thyself also in the Lord; and He shall give thee the desires of thine heart. (5) Commit thy ways unto the Lord; trust also in Him and he shall bring it to pass. (6) And he shall bring forth thy righteousness as the light and thy judgement as the noonday. (7) Rest in the Lord, and wait patiently on Him…."* Also verses 8 and 23-27. **Verse 8: *"Cease from anger, and forsake wrath: fret not thyself in any wise to do evil"*.

I made a copy of verses 3-7, cut them out and taped them to the corner of my desk at work to refer to them thru the day. I read them at home. Over and over, and over, and over. I learned them and repeated them to myself during the day to keep depression at bay. Before long when I had a bad thought go through my head like a lightning bolt I would tell myself *"STOP IT"* and *"I trust you Lord"*. These repetitions became a type of mantra to me and I made them my guide. I said *"I trust you Lord"* many times during the day for many different thoughts. Doing this gave me a mental focus on God's provision and mercy for me which helped me to keep thoughts away from me that were associated with things that caused my anxieties and depression.

I had always said God put me at the dealership and would remove me when He deemed it time for me to go. After eighteen years that happened. In the last year the stress got so bad I woke up not wanting to go to work. The days passed slowly. I marked them off the calendar. About 7 years ago, on 31 December, I quit work. I applied for my social security. This of course gave me some anxiety because I would not be getting a pay check anymore. Again, *"I trust you Lord to provide all my needs"*. After a few months, I settled down, relaxed, and was able to start enjoying my life without stress caused work. My time was mine without alarm clocks. Get up when I wanted, lie down when I wanted; time without any authority over me, controlling me other than God.

My psychiatrist recommended me going to a non-VA counseling facility in a group session. At that time my anxiety was worse and caused shaking in my hands so bad I couldn't write in cursive – I had a difficult time even printing. She felt this would help me considerably. I agreed to try it. The sessions were structured into two groups. One for general anxiety and depression and the second for Post-Traumatic Stress, anger management and drug/alcohol abuse. I was in the first group. Three times a week, three hours per day for eight weeks. Each week a psychiatrist at the facility met one time with each person once a week for progress and recommendations.

There were a few specific things that I focused on to achieve control of my issues, though there were many techniques presented to help but those or any other technique would be to no avail if the hearer didn't apply them to his or her daily life to improve. A major truth in all these issues is that nobody in the sessions got to the bad state they found themselves in overnight. Through the years I plead ignorance of some of it to myself or just dealt with it as best I could. *The longer anxiety and depression are allowed to continue the worse it becomes.* These are parasites that attack the very soul of man and sap his will to live. *Getting no treatment leads to worse anxiety. It doesn't get better on its 'own.* Once you have it, it never goes away. You always have it. *The only way to achieve control is to daily apply techniques to combat it. Every day.* Keep in mind I continued praying, repeating the psalm 37 verses to myself, telling the Lord I trust you or I trust in you, And telling myself, when I had a negative thought, Stop It!.

One of the most important things I did to achieve control is an old and well used military stratagem. You must know your enemy in order to defeat him; learn his ways and tactics used to attack you, harm you and destroy you if you allow him to. *The first objective to accomplish is to analyze each situation when you have had an anxiety or panic attack, as well as a depressive attack.* By this I mean think about the circumstances happening when it occurred, i.e., *try to determine What Are The Triggers, specifically, that caused the anxiety reaction. Only after identifying these triggers can you begin to develop a "plan of attack" to stop them.* After I discovered my "triggers" I used the technique of situational placement thinking. That means *(1) I would frequently picture myself in a situation where normally an attack would occur, then (2) ask myself "is my minds subconscious reaction (the burning muscles, increased respiration and heart rate, muscle weakness, flushing, nausea, tremors/shaking, etc) the response that a "normal person" would have. Of course the answer is no.*

Then (3) I would imagine myself in the same trigger situation but this time without the anxiety response. Just me in the situation doing a specific thing but calmly, at ease, relaxed from the first part to the last until the issue or condition is completed without fear.

The triggers (know the enemy) gave me a way to actually mentally go on the offensive attack against those triggers and mitigate their effect. It is a technique that must be practiced over and over. By it you will gain confidence. *You are specifically reprogramming your brain-your subconscious to respond to the triggers in a normal way rather than an abnormal and destructive way.*

I will share one specific way I used. I thought of the situations and triggers as flying dragons seeking to attack and destroy me. To protect my thoughts against the dragons I made a mental, imagined defensive transparent bubble around me. This meant the dragons, when attacking could not touch me. I was safe. But the next step was courageous and bold. No one can maintain just defense all the time, because those "triggers" or dragons are always attacking. *They never stop.* I imagined stepping outside of my bubble of safety with weapons. As the trigger dragons flew I imagined shooting them with the weapons, killing them causing the attacks to stop. I then returned to the safety of the bubble. The bubble always remains. This imagining technique proved successful albeit slowly. Repetition of the exercise was and remains necessary for me even now.

Another effective technique specific to the anxiety and panic attacks is very fast total relaxation of arms, legs, torso muscles to shut down the anxiety reactions. Relaxation also slows fast breathing and heartbeat and can stop tremors.

In the group sessions I was a little better than those in the session at this as I had learned self-hypnosis in college back in 1971. I never thought it would be such a readily available weapon to fight my attacks, but it came in very handy, very quickly and effectively. The relaxation technique requires practice. You get to a quiet place, recline if possible, or use a comfortable chair. Close your eyes, clear your mind of thoughts [which took me several weeks to achieve], and tell each muscle group to relax. One by one. Start with each leg, then each hand and arm. Next the torso, then the neck, head, and face. Don't hold yourself back. Your breathing will slow – keep going. With me I can change my breathing from about 14-18 times a minute down to 4 or 5. I do not hold my breath I just don't need to breathe. The intervals between needing to breathe increases and breathing is shallow. My heartrate has been dropped from around normal 62 a minute to around 54 or so. To do this you have to "let yourself go" – totally relaxed, repeating relax more and more on each muscle group. At some point I have gotten relaxed enough to experience a floating sensation as if I am floating down into total relaxation or sleep as a feather might float. I may count backwards from 10 to zero. It really works and you may even go to sleep. Waking you are much more relaxed and feel refreshed. This type technique can be self- taught but more information could be found in a public library if one wished to pursue it.

Above all other techniques though is FAITH. I asked the Lord to help me commit myself to him (from Psalm 37) and trust also in Him. I needed to hear him speak to me. Praying I asked he give me ears to hear his voice, eyes to see his blessings, and a tongue (voice) to give thanks unto him for it all. Learning to hear Him is a matter of tuning in. When **God speaks he does it in a whisper, as a quiet thought flashing through your mind.** As an example, one Saturday I was hauling off some trash. On the way I drove past several yard sale signs, but passing one in particular, I heard a thought that said "turn here-go around the block back to that yard sale". I did. Just happens that a good friend of mine (Bill) was furnishing a new sewing building for his wife because the old one was destroyed by Hurricane Michael in 2018 [During the storm I didn't have a panic attack].When I arrived at the sale there were 2 sections of used countertop that would be perfect for her to put sewing machines on. I asked how much? The owner said "nothing-just take them. You can have them." Wow. I called my friend and told him. His wife was very excited about it. *Here again is God providing a need.* All I had previously said to them was used countertops work well because that's what I used when my wife and I made a sewing building for her.

PEACE ATTAINED

So then, for me my journey is over, though I remain vigilant about fighting the ongoing small skirmishes that occur from time to time with anxiety for me. Thankfully there are no more great and difficult battles against the triggers – those dragons that plagued me for so many years; those unseen enemies that had conquered me - nearly ruined me, resulting in "the pit" of darkest depression, full of anxieties and panic. I believe others can conquer the evils of the mind and subconscious, but it takes strength, determination and effort.

<u>People do what they want to do.</u> Thankfully sometimes they do more, much more but cannot do those good things alone. I have, by the journey into the pit and the struggle to climb out, the determination to be free of the demons that had haunted me for so long, to have killed the giant spiders, defeated the monsters and invaders, have fought and vanquished the evil that was within me and now have acquired peace within myself, peach with others, and peace with my lord and savior Jesus Christ. The "being out of control" issue is no longer an issue because I trust God who is always in control, therefore no anxiety.

To achieve this end, the end that I believe God intended me to achieve was done by medicine, by counseling, *and most of all by Faith.* I no longer take pills for depression, nightmares, or anxiety. My tremors have stopped and I write again. I do still take medication for my vertigo and have to deal with that dragon. This journey was not a cure all, heal all. The path God chose for me to become the Christian I now am has accomplished its' work. Would I change anything I went through? A resounding NO! Was the hardship and battle worth the price? ABSOLUTELY! If any part of my journey had been different I wouldn't be as I am now. Psalm 37 was there when I needed it and is true. "And I will bring forth your righteousness as the light and thy judgement as the noonday"! In the Old Testament Joseph had to go through many hardships-sold into slavery, put in prison, but eventually became the second most powerful person in the world of Egypt thus saving Egypt and the Hebrew nation from starvation. This took thirteen years. He had to undergo all the hardship in order to be molded into the man able to achieve those things God intended for him to accomplish. God has molded me into the Christian I now am. For without the pit I would never have written this book.

The Enemy is Fear…God has many answers for that in his Word. He is able to deliver. Look at **Joshua 1:9:"Have not I commanded thee? Be strong and of good courage; be not afraid, neither be thou dismayed: for the Lord thy God goeth with thee whithersoever thou goest".**Another: **II Timothy 1:7 "For God hath not given us the spirit of fear, but of power, and of love, and of a sound mind".**

There is a path to achieving peace. One part of it is learning to be content with what you have or what you do: I ask three things of the Lord – My Lord –each day. (1) Strength to walk in (follow) his ways (2) Mental awareness to keep his commandments (all 10) because no man can do so without

God's help and (3) that I sin not against him. By seriously believing and *applying* these to my life every day I have learned to *Give Thanks to the Lord for what I have*. Paul wrote in Phillipians 4:11:*"Not that I speak in respect of want: for I have learned, in whatsoever state I am, therewith to be content"*. For desiring something more expensive, bigger, better, younger, prettier leads to temptation, which in turn causes conflict and turmoil within the mind, body and soul. This is coveting. The 10th commandment: "thou shalt not covet...". Romans 7:7 I had not known lust (the desire for the things of the world), except the law (commandment) says "Thou shalt not covet".Trust in God for all things and be content with what you have-with what God has given you. To desire not the things of the world is better for you mentally and physically. God will supply all your needs..To be free of this and have contentment is to be without conflict and turmoil, and therefore *Peace.:"I waited patiently for the Lord; and he inclined unto me, and heard my cry. He brought me up also out of an horrible pit, out of the miry clay, and set my feet upon a rock, and established my goings. And he hath put a new song in my mouth, even praise unto our God... Blessed is that man that maketh the Lord his trust..." (Psalm 40:1-4, 11). "For none of us liveth to himself, and no man dieth to himself. For whether we live, we live unto the Lord; and whether we die, we die unto the Lord: whether we live therefore, or die, we are the Lord's" (Romans 14:7-8). Therefore "Trust in the Lord with all thine heart; and lean not to thine own understanding. In all thy ways acknowledge Him, and He shall direct thy paths. Be not wise in thine own eyes: fear the Lord (reverence Him), and depart from evil. It shall be health to thy naval and marrow to thy bones" (Proverbs 3:5-8).*

Only God can give peace but it sometimes does not come without a price. Christ said *"Peace I leave with you, my peace I give unto you, not as the world giveth, give I unto you. Let not your heart be troubled, neither let it be afraid"* (John 14:27).

Every life is created by God. Every life was endowed with a soul when it was created. By the grace of Almighty God and his planned journey for me into and out of the pit – a terrible price was required of me -he has guided me, shown mercy to me and not withheld His lovingkindness. ***HE*** *has allowed me an immeasurable blessing of his Peace. Now I have no fear of lack of control of my life because I have committed my life to Christ and depend on Him to control it. Therefore I have no worries. My God is able to accomplish anything I need. It's a freedom I never imagined having.*

Matthew 7:7-8 "Ask, and it shall be given you; seek, and ye shall find; knock and it shall be opened unto you: For every one that asketh receiveth; and thee that seeketh findeth; and to him that knocketh it shall be opened."

Matthew 6:33 "But seek ye first the kingdom of God, and his righteousness; and all these things shall be added unto you. Take no thought for the morrow: for the morrow shall take thought for the things of itself. Sufficient unto the day is the evil thereof."

You may be in your own journey now, or may have a journey to make, unknown to you. If so, consider that I have gone through it and survived; I have become better by it. Only faith in God and His son the Lord Jesus Christ, Yeshua, can deliver you and give you PEACE!! I pray he will do so.

www.ingramcontent.com/pod-product-compliance
Lightning Source LLC
Chambersburg PA
CBHW070451130626
46553CB00006B/2357